Praise for Epic Life

*George takes one of the most ... ... vid,
and tells a story that demons... ... e
and promise to us as Christi... ... you
can hear his persistence and ... ... word on every
page as he shares this important story. This is a beautifully written
book that will help us all understand the meaning of living an
epic life."*

*– Geoff Duncan
Lt. Governor of Georgia*

*"Pastor George Dillard shares the compelling story of David,
'a man after God's own heart,' offering real-life perspectives for
parents, spouses, and members of the community. With a reminder
to trust in God's Word despite feelings of fear and uncertainty,
EPIC LIFE shares a message of courage and forgiveness essential
for today's society."*

*– Jameka Reese Character
Character Consulting, Business Owner*

*"This book takes the classic story of David and shares practical
insights from some new perspectives that are relevant to our
modern times. George has challenged us all to lead an epic life."*

*– Darren Key
CEO of Christian Financial Resources*

*"So beautifully written! I loved every bit of this amazing book. In
it, Pastor George captures the life of King David in a way that is
like no other; his words touched my heart, a definite must-read,
and re-read for anyone searching for an epic life with Christ!"*

*– Zoëy Iffland
Student*

LifeCast Publishing
A ministry of Peachtree City Christian Church
500 Kedron Drive
Peachtree City, GA 30269

www.PTC3.com

Written by George S. Dillard III, Ph.D.
Senior Editor: Michael Cooley
Assistant Editor and Layout: Theresa Howard
Readers: Reneé Dillard, Joy Hulsey, Rand Burton, Megan Smyth, Rex Wiseley

Cover by *life*together

ISBN: 9780692206898

Printed in the United States of America.

Visit info@ptc3.com or Amazon.com to order additional copies.

EPIC LIFE

The Life of King David

by George S. Dillard III, Ph.D.

I dedicate this book to my wife, Reneé,
my children and grandchildren: Tiffany,
Robert, Harper, Riar, Alexis, Stephen, and Stewart,
who are continually helping me as I try
to live the epic life.

EPIC LIFE

CONTENTS

EPIC LIFE

FOREWARD

I can't remember when I met George! Have you ever known someone for so long that you can't remember a time when he or she was not there? That's George! As soon as you meet him, you'll think you've always known him. I can't quite put my finger on it to describe it to you, but his outgoing personality really makes a lasting impression. George is the kind of guy who helps people get where they need to go. George takes time to invest in conversation with a genuine interest in you. He's a seasoned "people" professional, and he's aware of the challenges and discouragement high-performing people face.

The day George told me of his genuine interest in writing a book about the life of David, I asked myself why. I knew I was supposed to think about David like true "fans" of David think of him, but I struggled with the part about him being a man after God's own heart. So, I read his biography from 1 & 2 Samuel through 1 Kings. The remarkable story of David and Goliath has impressed me from my childhood, but have you read the rest of his story? This man is no role model; his life reads like a train-wreck. His children are more messed up than any reality TV family, or dysfunctional family of the week on a talk show. When David messes up, people die—sometimes many people.

A man after God's own heart? I didn't think so.

George and I talked about this more than a few times. Then one day, I changed my mind. Perhaps because George has worked with more than a few "David-types" in his career—people like me who have a passionate love for God but a talent for wandering off the beaten path and finding their way back through heartfelt and sometimes agonizing phases of repentance. George knows the secret to the epic life, knows it's found most profoundly in the events of David's life, and because he isn't put off by those of us who lose our way, he's passionate about showing others the way.

This book will help you see something in the life of David you may not have seen before. We look to Jesus as the example of one who lived a perfect life.

But, in the life of David we witness one more like the rest of us, who lived about as imperfectly as one can live, and yet, God loved him and he loved God, and he knew how to repent and be restored over and over again. This book highlights events in David's life that will make you question how this king could ever be considered for the title of man after God's own heart. Keep reading, because this book will explain the one trait that propelled him to obtain a great relationship with God despite monumentally bad choices and heart-breaking consequences.

David is passionate about his love for God, and in this book, you'll learn about David's sincere desire to follow God and faithfully do what God wants him to do.

David wrote most of the 150 Psalms in the Bible. His display of love for God's Word and devotion to Him comes out in passages like Psalm 119:47-48:

> ". . . for I delight in Your commands because I love them. I lift up my hands to Your commands, which I love, and I meditate on Your decrees."

Here you'll learn why David was a man after God's own heart and why he was truly thankful to God in all places and at all times.

Anyone can say they are going to do something and may claim they will accomplish it despite any obstacles or adversity that may get in their way. Saying you desire to do something and sticking with it—over time, over obstacles, over adversity—now that's an entirely different thing than just "talk." George has faced his share of trouble too, and unanticipated obstacles were always present as he compiled and completed this book. He's invested in this story. It's been a long time coming.

You will find George's relentless passion and patience on every page. I invite you to go on the journey and let George assist you in understanding what living an epic life is all about.

Michael Cooley
Senior Editor

INTRODUCTION

What do you want out of life? Do you desire more? Would you like to live an epic life? Almost everyone thinks they want more out of life—to live a life filled with accomplishments, popularity, respect, and notoriety. Who wouldn't like to have a legacy that features the slaying of a giant? Perhaps the more interesting question, and one you may not have thought about, is, have you determined what an epic life looks like? Do you know what it means and what it takes to live a life you and others would consider epic? What is an epic life?

The word epic can function as either a noun or an adjective. The life of David is epic in both and coincides with the two ways we define the word. When used as an adjective, epic refers to a heroic story or something noble or grand with deeds of great valor requiring superhuman courage. As a noun, epic is a long poem, typically derived from ancient oral tradition, narrating the deeds and adventures of heroic or legendary figures or the history of a nation as in Milton's *Paradise Lost*.

Epic works from oral tradition are usually works of poetry or narrative that re-tell stories of heroic and legendary figures of a nation's history. However, the word epic has gradually come to mean long films, books, or other works portraying heroic stories and adventures covering several years, perhaps even a lifetime. The portion of the Hebrew Testament from 1 Samuel through 1 Kings 2:10, tells of the epic life of David—that's epic as a noun.

As an adjective, the word epic points to the unique attributes of a character who lived a heroic life on a grand scale. I don't believe any other than Jesus Christ (the most epic of all) stands out more in the great lives recorded not just in Scripture but in all of human history.

Nearly 3,000 years after David's time on earth, the nation of Israel flies a flag that bears the Star of David as its banner. David's life is filled with many profound moments, yet these extraordinary moments reveal the extremes of the strength of his character and the scandalous proportions of his epic failures. Scripture refuses to shy away from embarrassing moments, poor choices, and bad attitudes—the story of David's life possesses both epic victory and epic failure. The details in the Biblical account of King David are amazing. The writer of these passages has been inspired with a gift to "zoom in" to the events and include details at some points such as the number of stones in a young shepherd's hands and the emotions and reactions of the characters. At other points, the writer "zooms out" and jumps to the next scene without filling in parts of the story not essential for readers to know.

As you read the account of the life of David, I encourage you to follow along with me in the Scriptures. Imagine what David's life would look like as an epic motion picture production unfolding on the screen. I encourage you to "binge" on the reading as you would binge-watch a television series. There's much more drama and intrigue here than many of the most popular series you could watch on-demand over the weekend.

At times, I'll share my personal opinion that comes from my reactions, my assumptions, and perhaps even my imagination as I walk through the passages of these three books of Israel's history and the life of its greatest king. As you read the account of David's life with me, you may agree or disagree. I only ask that in the process, you view the story with fresh eyes.

It is said to get the maximum enjoyment from watching a movie or reading a novel we ought to suspend our disbelief. The *"suspension of disbelief"* means we willingly put aside our criticism—sacrifice the realism and logic we usually apply in our daily lives for the sake of enjoying a story. Many do not share my belief in the truth of Scripture. I'll ask you to turn off, or at least press the pause button, on your thoughts of the implausibility of this epic tale. You need not believe the historicity of events to appreciate the practical and moral teaching contained within its narrative. For those who believe that the Biblical account of David's life is a historical fact, I ask something from you as well. I also invite believers to embrace the narrative with fresh eyes—as if you have never read or heard the story of David before. If you begin to feel I take too many liberties, please stay with me. It is not my intention to distort the truth, but shine a spotlight on possibilities and aspects of the story that might be important to consider.

Only rarely do the pages of history reveal one who has lived a life with the epic proportions of King David. This great story seems to leap out at us with significance, giving us a glimpse into an extraordinary life of a single astonishing human being that amazes, captivates, and demands our attention. Consider this short book on the life of David as a journey. We'll

GET READY!

In the summer of 2015, The National Trust in Wales ran an advertisement looking for a shepherd (or shepherdess) to care for its flock of 1,600 sheep in the foothills of Snowdonia. The ad read, "Shepherd wanted. Must enjoy drizzle and loneliness. People who prefer the company of humans, or like to stay dry, need not apply." Days will be spent preventing the Welsh Mountain sheep from tumbling into bogs or tramping over sensitive hillside habitats such as upland heaths. "The role itself is truly the opportunity of a lifetime, but it is not for everyone," said Arwyn Owen, manager at the National Trust farm Hafod-y-Llan.

Today, at least in the Western world, most of us who are familiar with Biblical accounts of shepherds *"Keeping watch over their flocks at night"* (Luke 2:8B) don't think much about what it means to be a

He had made Saul king over Israel." Think about it; you have to mess things up in a pretty big way for God Himself to say something like this about you. The Lord's judgment against Saul breaks the heart of Samuel—Saul's friend and mentor.

Samuel is the prophet who anointed Saul as king over Israel. A prophet is a man raised by God to call His people to Him to repentance; it was the prophet's responsibility to teach the people God's laws and how to follow them. The work of all true prophets of all ages is to act as God's messenger and make His will known. God still raises prophets today who have the same responsibilities as in the time of Samuel—ministers and leaders of His Church, gifted to teach His people about Him. It has to be agonizing for our Father when someone who has surrendered their life to Him refuses to follow His direction. Unfortunately, we can't take anyone where they are not willing to go. It is heartbreaking to see lives crumbling, yet feel helpless because we can't make someone follow God. We can encourage them, we can help them, we can walk with them, but we can't force them. Here Samuel has to stand on the sideline and watch as Saul and Israel's world falls apart around them. Saul was a phenomenal human being who had great potential, but he squanders it all.

But the Lord doesn't allow Samuel to grieve over Saul very long. What happens next is a powerful lesson in how our ways are not the same as God's ways. The Lord doesn't look at things the way a man looks at things. Man looks at the outward appearance, but the Lord looks at the heart. God sent Samuel to find the man He had chosen, the man with a heart for Him, and that man just happened to be the youngest son of a man named Jesse.

Jesse is probably a little nervous to see Samuel on his doorstep asking if he can have a word with him. I think Jesse may have become even more concerned when Samuel tells him why he is there. All but one of Jesse's sons is in Saul's army. They fight alongside Saul against the Philistines. They are men of valor—impressive in their own right. Do you know how I know Jesse's sons are remarkable men? Think about this; they send David out to watch his father's sheep. While David is out there, he slays a bear and a lion with nothing except a strap of leather and a rock, but this does not seem to impress his brothers or his dad. It impresses the heck out of me, but they are like, so what, not a big deal; this guy is nothing to them because they are hardened, battle-trained men. But you know what, even they are scared when Samuel comes to town. Many things God asks us to do come with an element of fear. The book of Proverbs in the collected wisdom of the Hebrew Testament tells us to trust in the Lord. Proverbs 3:5-6 says,

> *Trust in the Lord with all your heart and lean not on your own understanding; in all your ways acknowledge Him, and He will make your paths straight.*

When Samuel comes to Jesse's home, Jesse brings all of his sons except for one—his youngest, David, who is "*tending sheep*" (1 Samuel 16:11). I wonder if Jesse's family even considers David as one who could be chosen. It seems everyone is confident David does not have what it would take to meet the qualifications.

First, Samuel looks at the eldest son, Eliab. Eliab must have been tall and handsome, possibly the most outgoing son—the leader of the pack, the pick of the litter. But God says, not him. Then Samuel moves down the line from one son to the next, then the next, and none of them are God's choice. When he gets to whom he thinks is the last son and the Lord has not selected any of them, Samuel looks at Jesse and asks if he has any more boys. His words are the equivalent of, is this all you've got? Are you holding out on me?

The truth comes out as Jesse explains the youngest son is tending the sheep, but, look, it can't be him. Samuel says he's not going to sit down until Jesse brings his youngest son. He needs to get him because God told him He is going to anoint a king, so it must be this youngest one. Sure enough, the little shepherd boy David was God's choice. Samuel anoints David in front of all his brothers, and, *"...from that day on the Spirit of the Lord came upon David in power"* (1 Samuel 16:13B).

Following his encounter with the prophet Samuel, it must have been hard for David; after all, he had been anointed a king. He had to know he was different, gifted and talented, and must have been restless and eager to do something. Yet, how could he know what his real purpose in life would be? At this time in young David's life, returning to the care of sheep must have been dull and unimportant—indeed a job for a boy, not a king. And where are his brothers? They are in a battle, standing at the front lines defending the nation against the army of Philistines.

Why wasn't David getting military training? Why wasn't he enrolled in the pre-military training program of the Israeli Defense Forces? He must have longed to be near the front lines of battle like his brothers. But God put him in a place that prepared him for the future, a place with more action than the front lines. Unlike the shepherds in Wales, there were predators in the Middle East—wild animals dwelt in that region.

Yes, being a shepherd could be annoying, but it had its moments of excitement. With God's help, David defends the flock against two enemies he could not reason with: a lion and a bear. He conquers both and lives to tell about it and probably has no idea the wilderness proves to be a better training ground than the front line. Ironically, nothing is happening there but talk, a lot of smack-talk going back and forth—not much tactical warfare. One of the keys to living an epic life is realizing you can be prepared, shaped, and molded wherever you are stationed in life. We are sometimes called to grow where we are planted. David is being prepared by being left at home.

There was a time in my ministry when I wanted to go somewhere else. Each day I grew more discontented and convinced myself my efforts were failing. My wife, Reneé, asked me, "Why don't you just try to be happy with the situation?" When I thought about it and realized the truth contained in Renee's question, everything turned around. Rather than wanting something different, I realized the unique opportunity standing right in front of me. I began to thrive rather than survive. God opened up floodgates and gave me a renewed passion I may have missed if I had kept trying to strive without His strength. I needed to become more like David; I needed to become an obedient servant rather than a man seeking more power and authority.

Today, more than ever before, people seek and demand more. We want more income, more leisure time, longer and more extravagant vacations, and may wrongly believe ourselves to be entitled to these things and pursue them with high intensity. What we really ought to desire with all the energy we can muster is a relationship with God. Jesus taught us not to worry about material possessions but to seek those things that are higher.

> *"Do not store up for yourselves treasures on earth, where moth and rust destroy, and where thieves break in and steal. But store up for yourselves treasures in heaven, where moth and rust do not destroy, and where thieves do not break in and steal. For where your treasure is, there your heart will be also."*
>
> —Matthew 6:19-21

David sought to have a relationship with God; this is why he is a fascinating follower of God. Beginning in 1 Samuel 16, we read as God seeks out David, and David returns to Him many times; he falls and then gets back up. He falls; God lifts him back up. He falls again, and God—the Good Shepherd—remains faithful. David, like us, is full of imperfection that makes him prone to wandering off into the wilderness of the flesh. Yet, God describes David as *"a man after His own heart"* (1 Samuel 13:14). He is not a flawless man, but a man full of flaws. He is the man who will write,

> *You do not delight in sacrifice, or I would bring it; You do not take pleasure in burnt offerings. The sacrifices of God are a broken spirit; a broken and contrite heart, O God, You will not despise.*
> —Psalm 51:16-17

What makes the difference is a heart that is surrendered to God and understands that it cannot live without a relationship with Him. When it comes to what matters most to God, it is the heart that drives us.

God tells us where to go and what to do; Jesus says, *"Come, follow Me"* (Matthew 4:19), and the faithful follow His lead. We are sometimes asked to go into fearful places, but Jesus doesn't say, "Hey, go over there, and if you get into trouble, call on Me, and I'll be there." He doesn't even tell us to take Him along with us just in case we run into trouble, and He will handle it. Jesus says He will go first, and we are to follow Him and not worry about it. He promises to be with us. We can have faith that He is faithful to keep His promise, wherever He leads.

For Saul, who has stopped following God, things only get worse. *"Now the Spirit of the Lord departed from Saul"* (1 Samuel 16:14a). Scripture tells us Saul becomes tormented, and ironically Saul's servants suggest a little music therapy for the king. Who ends up getting the job? David, of course. At first, Saul loves David and keeps him in his service, even giving him the responsibility of being his armor-bearer. David plays for Saul whenever he feels tormented because God's Spirit has left him. Unfortunately, David and Saul's relationship soon begins to fall apart, as we will see in the following chapters.

Have you ever felt the way David must have as he sat watching over his father's sheep? Have you ever wondered about your purpose and meaning in life? David may not have realized what he was born to do, but that didn't stop him from following what he knew God wanted. What if there is one thing you are born to do, and you miss it because you choose not to follow where God leads?

EPIC LIFE

GOD'S INSTRUMENT

The ancient world pressed high numbers of the male population into the business of war. No one knew how to push forward the policy of war better than the Greeks and Romans. Ancient historians continuously discussed the Persian Wars, the Peloponnesian War, and the Punic Wars. The empire with the most massive numbers of men tended to win. Not only did Greek and Roman empires rely heavily on deploying the most formidable infantry to achieve victory, but they also used shock tactics. There's power in using sheer psychological impressions to defeat an enemy taken by surprise.

The stability of troops in the field depends on the order maintained by their commander. The courage of the infantry is a very fragile thing. Having an advantage of strength beyond the troops themselves is a definite asset. One of my favorite shock tactics from the ancient world is the elephant. Elephants are like living tanks. In the battle of Heraclea, Roman forces were in shock and awe at the charging elephants with towers containing archers spraying arrows out windows on each side. The hope was to bring shock and demoralize the troops—especially the commanders—with fear and trembling at their show of force.

Many years before the enemies of the Romans brought elephants to the battlefield; the Philistine army brought something different to shock the Israelites. One day in the early phase of posturing before the start of the actual battle, the Philistines sent out a nine-and-a-half-foot tall giant named Goliath.

I believe the sheer magnitude of Goliath's presence often escapes us. Close your eyes and try to picture a man who would stand three feet taller than the most massive NFL lineman whose shoulders are almost four-feet wide. Now consider that the average Israelite is a mere four-feet, six-inches tall. Goliath is twice anyone's size in Israel, including Saul, their champion.

Without hesitation, I tell you the sight of Goliath strikes fear in the hearts of the enemies of the Philistines; he is the vision of a pure warrior. Also, consider a fact that would be well known from childhood—Goliath had been trained in the art of war. To battle, he brings with him an impressive shield, a magnificent sword, a spear, and a javelin; he is entirely ready to win!

No one in Israel is ready, much less willing, to enter the valley of death. I wonder if the thought of this day reverberated in David's mind as he penned the words that would become part of what we know as The 23rd Psalm, *"Even though I walk through the valley of the shadow of death, I will fear no evil, for You are with me."* Goliath is not a shy one, nor does he appear to have any fear of speaking before a live audience. He teases them; he taunts them; he makes fun of them; he disrespects them, all the while he is mocking the name of the Living God.

In today's language, he might say, Come on! Where's this God of yours? Can He not show Himself? Let's see Him! Where's He at? (1 Samuel 18:8-10, paraphrase). He taunts them and challenges them to have their Deity show up. Israel insists their God is the One True God, and Goliath is goading them by asking where He is.

After some days of hearing these taunts, with no appearance by Israel's God, the smack-talking Goliath changes his approach as if to say, Hey, since your God is a no-show, shouldn't one of you brave fellows step up and at least defend His honor? Goliath knew no boundaries. He must grow impatient himself, *"For forty days the Philistine [Goliath] came forward every morning and evening and took his stand,"* hoping to provoke someone to anger, or any reaction at all (1 Samuel 17:8-17).

Then David arrives with supplies from his father for the fighters. This day wasn't a day anyone expected a grand happening would occur. Perhaps the sky was the same blue, dotted with clouds. It wasn't a day with any anticipation or electricity in the air. In tents, the many men rolled their pelts and hung their tethers. David *"reached the camp as the army was going out to its battle positions, shouting the war cry"* (1 Samuel 17:20в). David leaves his things with the keeper of supplies and runs out to meet his brothers. When he is talking with them, Goliath comes back into the center of the battlefield to issue his daily challenge: Fight me and lose—you belong to me. Fight me and win—you get the entire Philistine army (Paraphrase mine).

David looks around to see who is going out—he automatically assumes someone will. Why wouldn't he make this assumption? This beast of a man is taunting the Most High God. However, David is the only one who sees it that way. His love of God and faith in God in all circumstances take precedence over every other thought. You see, David doesn't yet realize he is the only one hearing the challenge. Can you imagine him standing there, bright-eyed and optimistic? He wants to be the first person to shake the hand of the man who will fight and slay a giant for the glory of God. He waits. His countenance falls. When there are no takers he simply cannot believe it. He waits a little bit longer, and his mood changes. He becomes angry and outspoken, but as he becomes louder in his protests one of his brothers approaches him and tells him to quiet down. But there's no quieting a man whose God has been mocked, who knows that his God is bigger than Goliath, bigger than the seas, the vast deserts, all of that which is encompassed in a marble-sized universe under one Almighty thumb.

David does something wholly human, and here is an important point: David cannot hold himself back. He has seen what God can do when He empowers His people and uses them to defeat a threat—like a lion or a bear. David determines that this giant is in the same category, and he knows this threat will be beaten that day. It is happening, and David announces that he'll accept the challenge of the enemy, whatever form or size the enemy comes in.

So, David makes up his mind—he can do this. He's done nearly the same thing before defending his father's flock. Only this time there is an audience, and the reputation of Israel and the One True God is on the line. The Philistines and their giant of a champion make David's blood boil, so he jumps into action. However, the demoralized troops are less than enthusiastic at his bravery.

Word of this reaches Saul, who sends for young David. Imagine Saul—on the fence-line between wisdom and the trappings of ego hearing such news. When David arrives, Saul takes one good look at him and assumes his men are having a bit of fun. Could this hobbit-like character be more than an armor bearer?

Saul decides to outfit young David with his immaculate armor, the weight of which would have been heavy even on Saul himself. We don't really know what Saul is thinking about David at this point. Because we are all so familiar with the story, the bizarre attitude of the king escapes us more quickly than someone hearing the story for the first time. What do you think would strike the ears of those hearing the story for the first time?

- The king does not forbid this shepherd boy from challenging the giant.
- The king does not assign the job to someone.
- The king does not accept the challenge (despite the fact he is a seasoned professional warrior himself).
- The king puts his armor on David.

The last one probably scores higher than all the others with its lack of reasoning. Why is the king putting any battle gear on a small shepherd boy who speaks out and volunteers to engage a giant in a one-on-one, to-the-death competition? Why is Saul permitting this action at all? What good can possibly be attained by watching the mocking army mock them even further, and then slice and dice a shepherd boy wearing the king's armor? This is a recipe for making things much worse than they were before. It defies logic. Possibly Saul is using this to prove a point: if David can't handle Saul's armor, how can he possibly hope to beat this overwhelming enemy?

However, it is at this point in the story when David does the unexpected. David does not care about defensive armor because he knows what no one else does. David is the only one in the Israelite camp who realizes the fight with Goliath is not going to be one-on-one. Through his experiences in life, David knows he is going to be more of an instrument of God than a warrior.

In many ways, the day Saul offers his armor to David is the same day Saul ceases to be a warrior—more specifically, Saul stops being a warrior for God. He misses the most significant opportunity of his life, and his life begins a downward spiral from which he will never recover. You see, this story is not just about the victory of David, but the surrender and self-defeating actions of the mighty warrior King Saul. The reality is that Saul could have been as equally victorious as David had he faced Goliath. In fact, as the king, it is his responsibility as the leader of his people to go out there in the first place. Instead, he passes on this opportunity and allows a young shepherd boy to meet the Philistine's champion. The regret he carries from that moment and the hatred born out of it will eventually destroy his life.

What ultimately hinders Saul's relationship with God is that he blames his failure back on God. Perhaps Saul thinks God should just let David perish down in that valley. As a strategist, he might figure the death of David would be better for Israel, as his subjects would realize all they need to do is join together. Or, perhaps having a nobody of a shepherd boy die is better than a mighty king slain.

As mentioned in the first part of this chapter, given the height of the average Israelite, it is quite possible the champion they sent out is roughly the same size as one of Goliath's legs. In other words, Goliath is very BIG. From what we know about David, the sword Goliath is carrying is likely as big as he is. Think about that for a second; this guy's sword is as big as David. How do you think David feels at this moment?

Chances are pretty good when David picks up that first stone; he looks out of the corner of his eye at Goliath, who is standing there in all his might and power with no idea what is about to happen. But David, however, is convinced that God will rule the day. This is why I have said for years, "Plan like it depends on you but live knowing it depends on God."

David brings glory to God by allowing himself to be used, time and time again, without running backward and hiding behind excuses and fear. He is alive in God and God in him. David faces down a bear and a lion because he knows that God has a plan; that though he cannot see the other side of the mountain, God can view the entire range from every angle. He knows God is doing something; all he has to do is trust Him.

Listen to what the Holy Spirit reveals to John. In 1 John 4:4B, *"...the One Who is in you is greater than the one who is in the world."* We might not know what the exact result will be when we face our giants, but we can know that the ultimate victory is ours. Jesus has conquered the last of our enemies: sin and death. Why should we be afraid? I can promise you that no giant we face is bigger than the wages of sin, the second death, and the regret that comes from backing down from challenges and obstacles. I know human nature, and I am reasonably sure that the final thoughts of those Israelite soldiers before they went to sleep at night were: I should have gone out there. I should have stood up for God. I should have got in the fight.

Rely on God; it changes everything. You will no longer see an overwhelming giant, but a mission to glorify and thank the One Who loves you enough to purchase you after He has already been your Creator. We need to commit not only to facing our giants but meeting them with the intent of overcoming them.

Goliath looks upon David as he comes at him with only a sling and some stones. Can you imagine this scene? At first, Goliath probably thinks it is a joke. One can easily imagine Goliath saying to himself: You've got to be kidding me, right? This kid doesn't even have a shield or a sword. What is he doing? Afterward, Goliath becomes angry at the whole spectacle by what he perceives as mocking. He asks David, *"Am I a dog, that you come to me with sticks?"* (1 Samuel 17:43). Then he seems to come to the place where he thinks one dead Israelite is as good as another, taunting David to *"Come here,"* he says, *"... and I'll give your flesh to the birds of the air and the beasts of the field!"* I love what happens next—David runs straight for Goliath. When everyone is running away or keeping a safe distance, David runs to the battle.

David does not adorn himself as a battle-trained warrior. Beating this giant seems impossible to others, but we must remember the giants we face have two objectives: to make God look bad and to keep us from doing what God wants us to do in the world. Giants will taunt us; they will attempt to grip us with paralyzing fear. That's no way to live. We need to face our giants. We don't know how it will play out, but we know that we will not be alone or without protection; God will provide the armor. Ephesians 6:13 says,

> *Therefore, put on the full armor of God, so that when the day of evil comes you may be able to stand your ground and then after you have done everything to stand.*

David put on that armor. In 1 Samuel 17:45-47 we read,

> *You come against me with sword and spear and*
> *javelin, but I come against you in the name*
> *of the Lord Almighty, the God of the armies of*
> *Israel, whom you have defied. This day the Lord*
> *will hand you over to me, and I'll strike you*
> *down and cut off your head. Today I will give*
> *the carcasses of the Philistine army to the birds of*
> *the air and the beasts of the earth and the whole*
> *world will know that there is a God in Israel. All*
> *those gathered here will know that it is not by*
> *sword or spear that the Lord saves; for the battle*
> *is the Lord's, and He will give all of you into our*
> *hands.*

So, we have a nearly ten-foot-tall giant on one side and a small boy with a leather sling and few stones on the other. (You don't see something like this every day!) David faces Goliath not as a soldier but as an instrument of power—the power of the Living God. Most, if not all of us, know David wins. He even removes the head of the giant with his own sword and holds it up. I'm sure the gaping open mouth of the pale and lifeless face of Goliath matches the same pale and courage-less gaping open mouths of the entire Philistine army.

What's the application in this story for us today? Well, maybe it is time we stopped running from the giants that challenge us. Perhaps we should face off with them and rely on God's power through us. Maybe it's time we begin running to the battle—toward our giants—facing them with reliance on the Living God. The lesson we should take away from this truth is that when we trust God, we cannot lose. The outcome may not be as we think it will be, however, when everything is entrusted to God, relying on His power ultimately results in victory.

Three-thousand years later, we are still talking about this battle between a shepherd boy and a giant. Let's stop for a moment, set the stage, and play this scene over again in our mind. Here's the wide-angle view of what is about to happen: The Philistine army is camped out on one side of the valley, with the Israelites camped on the opposite side. Between them, the expanse of the valley, with two mighty nations poised against one another. It was customary in those days for each side to send out their champion, ready to fight with a sword in hand and shield on the arm. Usually, these posturing contests were pretty evenly matched. Both champions would hold equally to the idea that training and preparation had given them all the tools needed for one to emerge victorious from the battle arena; both were also keenly aware only one would survive the battle.

Where does your courage come from? Courage is always based upon faith in something or someone. If we lack courage, it can only be due to a lack of faith. Some "giant" of some sort is taunting and mocking our faith in God, and we feel like the others on the field of battle that day, inadequate to stand up to what appears to our eyes as an impossible fight. Our fear immobilizes us.

We must remember that our battle is not with flesh and blood. Ephesians 6:12 points out that the giant we confront is the *"spiritual forces of evil in the heavenly realms."* Make no mistake, these giants are greater than we are and possess the ability to conquer our hearts, minds, and flesh, seemingly, like Goliath, they can destroy anyone who confronts them. But these giants fall just like Goliath when we draw our courage from God and bear in mind that our God is the same God of David, a faithful God who keeps His promises.

THE CHASE

It's tough being the underdog. I find great inspiration from underdog stories—those who do what they do best, fight the odds, push through the criticism, drive through the obstacles when the deck is stacked against them. One unsung hero is from the small town of Danville on the outskirts of the Commonwealth of Virginia.

During the racially challenging and turbulent period of the 1960s, Wendell Scott became the first African-American driver in the mostly white sport of NASCAR. Wendell is the first African-American winner of a Series Cup, and perhaps the first winner not permitted to take a victory lap. Instead, Buck Baker was flagged as the winner, given the trophy, and took the victory lap. After checking scorecards, the officials revealed Scott actually won the race. There's little doubt this "error" was not an error at all. This calculated move avoided a scene where a black driver would receive the kiss of congratulations from a white race queen. Yet, Wendell raced full-time from 1962 to 1971 at the top of the series, then called the Grand National.

NASCAR wanted Wendell to race, of course. They needed the expanded audience of African-Americans that an African-American driver would bring. They simply didn't want him to be the winner and get all the accolades. We see a similar situation with David and Saul. Saul didn't mind David leading the army into victory, but he grew increasingly jealous of how people talked about David's conquests.

Think about Saul's reaction when David killed Goliath. Instead of rejoicing in the victory, he immediately reacts with a strange question. He asks, Who is this kid? I believe, much like a modern-day politician, Saul considers possible damage to his reputation in the heat of the moment. Suddenly, it doesn't look good for him. One can imagine so much contempt toward David from Saul. After all, Saul is Israel's champion, her hero; he is the one that they used to sing about. Saul led Israel in many battles over the decades, and now this "kid" slays one person and swiftly grabs all the attention and honor as Israel's champion. Maybe Saul thinks he should have suited up and slain Goliath himself. But he can't do it over now; there is no going back.

Once I was looking at an original Jasper Johns painting, a friend of mine owned. The more I looked at it, the more I noticed the simplicity of this painting of an archery target painted different colors than usual. My friend asked me what I thought about it. I chuckled and said, "Honestly, I could have painted that." My friend smiled, looked at me and said, "Yes, but you didn't." I'm sure we can all recall times when we've thought to ourselves about the accomplishments of others and speculated how easy it would have been for us to do the same thing. Perhaps we regret those things we didn't do more than we feel pain over the things we tried to do and failed. Beware of this kind of regret and jealousy; it leads to dark places. A dark place is precisely where it took Saul.

Imagine if social media had existed back then. Saul might have reacted to a viral meme—a picture of Saul on one side and David on the other—underneath, the caption reads, *"Saul has slain his thousands, and David his tens of thousands"* (1 Samuel 18:7B). Perhaps you can imagine how Saul would have fumed watching the re-tweets, shares and likes stack up. Well, he wasn't looking at Instagram back then, but what happened could not have been worse for his ego. We read that Saul heard singing, tambourines and other instruments playing as people sang those words in the streets.

As Saul is harboring his anger, we read how a "harmful spirit" came upon him while David was in his house playing the lyre. Saul took his spear in his hand and,

> *hurled it, saying to himself, "I'll pin David to the wall." But David eluded him twice. Saul was afraid of David, because the Lord was with David but had left Saul.*
> —1 Samuel 18:11-12

David is already well known, but now that he is a military leader his men have the opportunity to get to know him, and the positive accolades spread via the Hebrew social media outlets of the day. We read how Israel and Judah love David, who both socializes and interacts well with the people and knows how to lead warriors to achieve great success on the battlefield.

Obviously, Saul is having a big ego problem with David—who is now the one in God's favor—in the picture. So Saul, perhaps wanting to seem as a grateful and benevolent king by the people, offers his oldest daughter Merab to David for his wife while all the time is thinking, *"I will not raise a hand against him. Let the Philistines do that!"* (1 Samuel 18:17B). But David doesn't quite understand how a king could offer him his daughter due to David's low social status. The daughter of the king is of noble birth, but David is from a working-class family and would not, under normal circumstances, be considered as a match for the king's daughter. So Saul ends up giving her to another man.

Later, Saul's younger daughter Michal falls in love with David, and Saul offers her to be his wife, but this time the offer comes with a condition—a rather unusual one—an opportunity to earn his position. David is told all the king wants for his daughter's hand is for David to kill one-hundred Philistines and return with their foreskins. I can only speculate about why Saul dreams up such a task for his future son-in-law; perhaps Saul thinks this task too dangerous and hopes David will die trying to fulfill the qualification. David, the overachiever, returns with two-hundred foreskins. Now Saul's fear of David only increases as a result of David's success. (I think I would want to be cautious around someone who went the "above and beyond" expectations of a strange task such as this.)

We know at this point David's popularity with the people, combined with his victories in battle, makes

Saul ever-increasingly jealous of him. Finally, we read, *"Saul told his son Jonathan and all the attendants to kill David"* (1 Samuel 19:1). Saul no longer seems to care about the loss of an inspirational and skilled military leader during a war; he wishes to eliminate a threat to his obviously weak ego. Saul has different priorities. Now, his personal jealousy creates a substantial problem for his son Jonathan, who cares a great deal about David. Jonathan finds himself caught in the middle between his loyalty and obedience to his father the king, and his devotion and love for a dear friend.

Jonathan warns David. This is no small act on Jonathan's part and shows how vital David was in his life. Jonathan says,

> *"My father Saul is looking for a chance to kill you. Be on your guard tomorrow morning; go into hiding and stay there. I will go out and stand with my father in the field where you are. I'll speak to him about you and will tell you what I find out."*
> —1 Samuel 19:2-3

The destructive thoughts of the king against David would have to wait a while. War intervenes and provides a distraction for a time. Everyone is focusing on the battles with the Philistines. As usual, David returns home the victor, and again Saul attempts to pin him to the wall with his spear. David eludes Saul's wrath another time and runs home. On arrival, he is greeted by his wife, Michal, who warns him, *"If you do not run for your life tonight, tomorrow you'll be killed"* (1 Samuel 19:11). She helps David escape out a window and arranges things to look as if David is sick in the bed. When Saul's hitmen fail to find David, Saul's anger grows even more.

You and I have an enemy. Our enemy has sadistic tendencies as well. The determination Saul displays as he attempts to end David's life should remind us of how our enemy works against us today as believers. The Body of Christ (the Church) has a "Saul"—an enemy seeking our destruction. In 1 Peter 5:8, we read, *"Be self-controlled and alert. Your enemy the devil prowls around like a roaring lion looking for someone to devour."* We need not be surprised when people we trust come at us to destroy us.

In his effort to escape from Saul's men, David flees to Samuel at Rama. When Saul learns of this, he sends men to capture David three times, but each time God intervenes. When none of his soldiers return, Saul finds out where David and Samual are and decides to capture David himself. God stops Saul as well. Then David flees to Saul's son Jonathan to plead his case. One last time Jonathan attempts to be the peacemaker between his father's rage and David. In

1 Samuel 20:18-23, David and Jonathan make an arrangement:

> *"Tomorrow is the New Moon festival. You will be missed, because your seat will be empty. The day after tomorrow, toward evening, go to the place where you hid when this trouble began, and wait by the stone Ezel. I will shoot three arrows to the side of it, as though I were shooting at a target. Then I will send a boy and say, 'Go, find the arrows.' If I say to him, 'Look, the arrows are on this side of you; bring them here,' then come, because as surely as the Lord lives, you are safe; there is no danger. But if I say to the boy, 'Look, the arrows are beyond you,' then you must go, because the Lord has sent you away. And about the matter you and I discussed—remember, the Lord is witness between you and me forever."*

At the feast that evening, David's seat is empty. Saul does not say anything this first evening. However, on the second night, Saul asks Jonathan, *"Why hasn't the son of Jesse come to the meal, either yesterday or today?"* (1 Samuel 20:27B). Jonathan answers and says,

> *"David earnestly asked me for permission to go to Bethlehem."* He said, *"Let me go, because our family is observing a sacrifice in town and my brother has ordered me to be there."*
>
> —1 Samuel 20:28-29

Saul reacts with anger saying,

"You son of a perverse and rebellious woman!
Don't I know that you have sided with the son of
Jesse to your own shame and to the shame of the
mother who bore you? As long as the son of Jesse
lives on this earth, neither you nor your kingdom
will be established. Now send and bring him to
me, for he must die!"
                    —1 Samuel 20:30-31

When Jonathan asks his father why David should be put to death, Saul hurls his spear at his own son. As long as Saul is alive, David's fate is sealed. Jonathan leaves the table in anger, and the next morning he shoots the arrow as planned. *"Isn't the arrow beyond you?"* Jonathan shouted, signaling for David to leave. *"Hurry! Go quickly! Don't stop!"* (1 Samuel 20:37). He shouts as if to the boy picking up his arrows, but really to David, for he fears his father's wrath against his friend. Jonathan gives his weapons to the boy and sends him away. As soon as he is gone, David rises from behind the stone heap and falls on his face, bowing to Jonathan three times, and they weep.

"Go in peace, for we have sworn friendship
with each other in the name of the Lord, saying,
"The Lord is witness between you and me, and
between your descendants and my descendants
forever."
                    —1 Samuel 20:42

This is such a powerful moment and a turning point between these two friends who must now go their separate ways. David could have killed Saul at any time in public or in private. His popularity was such that he would have prevailed in the civil war that may have broken out. Yet David chose to deal with this situation in a different way, God's way, and not the way of the world.

Saul's rage is immeasurable. When he finds the priests whom he trusts have helped David, he sentences them to death. Saul's men refuse to kill the priests, so Saul calls upon Doeg the Edomite; what follows is a massacre of eighty-five men wearing priestly vestments. In Nob, the city of the priests, Doeg kills men, women, children, nursing infants, oxen, donkeys, and sheep (I Samuel 22:6-19). Saul takes matters into his own hands, and his actions result in a horrifying tragedy that affects many generations to come. David, on the other hand, chooses wisely and handles the conflict by following the heart of God.

David's actions foreshadow the teachings of Jesus, who taught us to handle conflict in a much different manner than the world would. Jesus said when someone slaps you on the face, turn the other cheek, when they ask you for your shirt, give them your coat, and when they demand you walk a mile, go two. It is in this manner that when you forgive others, you will be forgiven (Matthew 5:38 ff.).

One day Saul takes three-thousand men from Israel into the wilderness to find David. He and his men are hiding in a cave when Saul comes in to relieve himself. David's men try to tell him this is the day the enemy has been delivered up to him, and he should do as he sees fit. David arises from the back of the cave and silently cuts off a corner of Saul's robe. But, even this is going too far for David,

> *Afterward, David was conscience stricken for having cut off a corner of his robe. He said to his men, "The Lord forbid that I should do such a thing to my master, the Lord's anointed, or lift my hand against him; for he is the anointed of the Lord."*
>
> —1 Samuel 24:5-6

David's words persuade his men not to attack Saul. Saul leaves the cave and goes on his way without seeing David. Then David emerges from the cave and cries out, *"My lord and my king!"* Saul turns and David bows and says,

> *"Why do you listen when men say, 'David is bent on harming you? This day you have seen with*

your own eyes how the Lord delivered you into my hands in the cave. Some urged me to kill you, but I spared you; I said, 'I will not lift my hand against my master, because he is the Lord's anointed.' See, my father, look at this piece of your robe in my hand! I cut off the corner of your robe but did not kill you. Now understand and recognize that I am not guilty of wrongdoing or rebellion. I have not wronged you, but you are hunting me down to take my life. May the Lord judge between you and me. And may the Lord avenge the wrongs you have done to me, but my hand will not touch you."

—1 Samuel 24:9-12

David is willing to handle this unbelievable conflict according to the will of God. He goes on to say to Saul,

"Against whom has the king of Israel come out? Whom are you pursuing? A dead dog? A flea? May the Lord be our Judge and decide between us. May He consider my cause and uphold it; may He vindicate me by delivering me from your hand."

Saul replies, *"Is that your voice, David my son?"* And he weeps aloud. He knows David has surpassed him again, this time in righteousness. Once again, David trusts God with the conflict. He does not go his own way, or the world's way, or the way others try to influence him. The turning point comes, and David chooses God's way (1 Samuel 24:14-16).

We see what David learns about conflict—this is a lesson we can learn as well. David does not ignore the situation or pretend it does not exist; he acknowledges the person. David doesn't confront Saul immediately, because confrontation is not always the best course of action, especially when someone is so angry with us that they cannot be reasoned with. I realize to some it might seem David did confront him immediately. Yet, I ask you to consider this possibility: David is a warrior king. He is used to making split-second decisions reacting in the moment. What I see here (as a person who has tendencies similar to these) is the exercise of restraint and thought, which—in my mind—requires patience. If we look at the narrative from a different perspective, we can see that patience is produced in the maturing of the fruit of the Spirit, which is love. David loves Saul even though he has been wronged by him, and above all, he loves God, which compels him to be patient. Handling this situation God's way doesn't mean a quick resolution. Finally, the most important takeaway from this episode in the life of David is the concept of forgiveness.

David exhibits a tremendous capacity to forgive. Among human beings, the forgiveness of this magnitude is rare. We read in Romans 5:8, *"But God demonstrates His own love for us in this: While we were still sinners, Christ died for us."* Forgiveness is an attribute familiar and close to the heart of God. David possesses forgiveness and patience that only a few people in history have attained. However, Saul allows his toxic thoughts to bear the fruit of destructive behaviors. David, while a victim of Saul's outrageous actions, remains calm and confident. We have a clue as to what David must have been thinking when we read his Psalms. We know he wrote some of those Psalms during the time when Saul directed his unbearable and irrational rage at him (see Psalms 56-58). It is beneficial to us if we keep this in mind when reading the account of David. Here we have a witness to the personal thoughts and prayers of one whose confidence, love, and loyalty to God surpasses comprehension.

As already mentioned, it is difficult to relate to David's measure of confidence and his love for God. David's faith makes him more than courageous. With such a firm and loving heart for God, it might seem that someone like David possesses the heart of a saint. He lives a life of unimaginable righteousness and purity beyond anyone before or after. David shows great rage at the giant Goliath who defies and defiles the name of his God, but he keeps a presence of mind and a respectful, patient attitude when dealing with Saul, who has wronged and attacked him. David appears to be a living saint! However, as we will see moving forward, David is about as far from being a saint as anyone. On the one hand, we see him having a spotless reputation and being an amazing example of moral fortitude; on the other, we see a man who takes matters into his own hands, defies God and deeply hurts his own family.

The descriptions, stories and songs about David are varied and intriguing—all which make the question of David being a man after God's own heart even more interesting. We have seen some examples that give us a little insight into what that might mean. Let's keep looking to find out why the Scripture describes him in this way.

EPIC LIFE

THE WRONG PLACE
AND TIME

Before we go further in the Biblical account of David, I want to remind you that we ought to regard Holy Scripture—the Word of God—as more than just a religious book or words on a page. At times the message is oh too human and found in small, very significant statements. In 2 Samuel 11:1, we read,

> *In the spring, at that time when kings go off to war, David sent Joab out with the king's men and the whole Israelite army. They destroyed the Ammonites and besieged Rabbah. But David remained in Jerusalem.*

In this passage, you'll notice two critical statements. The first statement I want us to look at is, "*at the time when kings go off to war.*" The Bible is telling us that David stayed behind rather than going to war as he should have. The implication of the passage indicates that the appropriate and customary place for the king during this time is away with the troops—with his army. The king holds the ultimate position of leadership in the nation, and as the nation's leader, he should have been leading by example. What impression does David leave by staying home? What effect do his actions have on the morale of the warriors and their families when they hear the king is not with the troops? Instead, he's sleeping in the comfort of his bed. The Scripture passage makes it clear David is home when explicitly mentioning that he remains in Jerusalem. This news is not fake or opinion, but such news would burn bitter fires of resentment among every citizen of the nation.

The David we now confront differs significantly from the one we read about in the last chapter. This version of David (David 2.0) is not an upgrade. This David doesn't spend time listening to the heart of God but following his own desires and comfort. When we stop listening to God and begin delegating tasks we should do ourselves; the results will not be favorable for us. This David fails to download the courage and righteous indignation of David 1.0. We now have a David who is not where he is supposed to be—even worse; he's where he should not be.

One evening David goes up to the rooftop, and as he is looking out over the city he sees a woman bathing.

She is stunning. We don't know if he lingers or not, but we do know he does something much worse; he sends someone to find out who she is and then has his messengers go get her. Her name is Bathsheba, daughter of Eliam and the wife of Uriah the Hittite, one of the men David sent off to war. While Uriah is out fighting the Ammonites, David is watching his wife, Bathsheba, take a bath. When we are out of God's will, our poor choices become terrible choices. We make mistakes, no matter how hard we try, but we can avoid creating absolute disasters. David didn't stay home in Jerusalem and away from the battlefield to have an affair. Perhaps, because of who he truly is, he has difficulty sleeping in his comfortable bed.

Looking at naked women bathing is definitely a wrong choice. However, if we are honest, most men would not be able to refrain from looking at such a sight—even if just for a moment. But this does not mean he has to keep looking; he has the option of turning away. We can prevent our wrong choices from becoming even worse decisions.

Unfortunately, David decides to go the worst decision route. Instead of just staying on the roof looking at her, he sends a messenger to bring her back to him. I think it is a safe assumption that this invitation is not made the very first night. At least, I would like to think that there are a few nights of contemplation before he summons her. Either way, David's actions go from a poor choice to a terrible decision of sexual immorality.

> *"Stay away from the lust of the flesh, the lust of the eyes, and the boastful pride of life, all of these things that will destroy you."*
> —1 John 2:16 (CEV)

All sins are equal, but sexual immorality affects the body and the soul, here and now. It also drives David to disregard God completely. He either fails to understand the consequences of giving in to this temptation, or he doesn't care; either way, the results are the same.

The Word of God consistently warns us about temptation and our inability to resist sin on our own. When temptation shouts in our ear, we can still hear the small voice of wisdom. Wisdom would have said, "turn around; go back inside and forget what you saw." David could have avoided making a terrible decision by resisting the urge to keep looking and rationalize, but he probably lingers. We can resist temptation by removing ourselves as quickly as possible from situations where we may be vulnerable. When we settle with corruption, we reap destruction.

As a pastor, one of the most frequent questions I hear people ask about God is, how do we know His will for us? We know His will when we are in communion with Him and allow Him to direct our choices from moment to moment. Only through His strength can we overcome the sometimes overwhelming force of temptation and the selfish, self-serving person we quickly become.

Bathsheba's husband, Uriah, is one of the outstanding men in David's army. But, David isn't thinking about the effect his actions will have on Uriah or Joab. David selfishly corrupts Bathsheba through an illicit affair, and she becomes pregnant with his child. First, David tries to cover it up. When that doesn't work out as he planned, he decides to arrange Uriah's death on the front lines. David tells Joab to leave Uriah exposed at the height of an intense battle. No decisions are made in a vacuum; all of our choices affect other people as well as ourselves.

Without God's guidance, David single-handedly makes all of these bad choices and attempts to cover them up with even worse decisions. He does not confess, nor does he seek redemption or forgiveness for his actions—he thinks he knows best. When we cease to follow God, we lose touch with reality. We reach a point where we believe sin is a viable option; then all the other things start slipping behind; suddenly, murder, lying, and deceit become possibilities open to us. I'm confident that the pregnant Bathsheba living in the house of David does not go unnoticed by his subjects, or by God. However, David seems to be above it all. Who is going to say anything to him?

In 2 Samuel 12:1–13, God sends Nathan to David with a parable. Nathan tells David about a rich man in the kingdom who has about as much money as David does; his pastures are so full of sheep they appear to be covered with snow. He tells David that the rich man's neighbor is a poor but honest man with high integrity. Nathan explains the poor man's prize possession is one little ewe lamb that he has owned since its birth. The man raised it as if it were his child; he plays with it and even sleeps with it in his arms. Nathan then tells David that the rich man decides to have a party and sends his servants to the poor man's house to take his precious lamb to serve the guests.

David becomes furious when he hears this story. He leaps off his throne and issues all sorts of threats against the rich man, demanding he deserves to die and should pay for that lamb four times over because he did such a thing. Nathan then tells David to look no further, *"you are the man!"* (2 Samuel 12:7). Nathan is talking about David, who then realizes his sin; the man of high integrity is Uriah the Hittite— the lamb, of course, is Bathsheba.

Scripture records the consequences of David's action in 2 Samuel 12:7–15, *"Then Nathan said to David, "You are the man! This is what the Lord, the God of Israel, says: 'I anointed you king over Israel and I delivered you from the hand of Saul. I gave your master's wives into your arms. I gave you the house of Israel and Judah. And if all this had been too little, I would have given you even more. Why did you despise the Word of the Lord by doing what is evil in His eyes? You struck down Uriah the Hittite with the sword and took his wife to be your own. You killed him with the sword of the Ammonites. Now, therefore, the sword will never depart from your house, because you despised Me and took the wife of Uriah the Hittite to be your own.' "This is what the Lord says: 'Out of your own household I am going to bring calamity upon you. Before your very eyes I will take your wives and give them to one who is close to you, and he will lie with your wives in broad daylight. You did it in secret, but I will do this thing in broad daylight before all Israel.'" Then David said to Nathan, "I have sinned against the Lord." Nathan replied, "The Lord has taken away your sin. You are not going to die. But because by doing this you have made the enemies of the Lord show utter contempt, the son born to you will die."*

After Nathan had gone home, the Lord struck the child that Uriah's wife had borne to David, and he became ill.

Nathan confronts David's selfishness and his unwillingness to flee from sin when he has the chance. Perhaps David, like many of us, feel we have a sense of entitlement. But we all will stand before God, any chance of redemption that we have is through surrender to Him as the Living God. There is no standing still in life. We are either moving toward God or moving away from Him. When we recognize we have made bad choices and we hear the alarms going off, we need to understand this is the moment we should heed the warnings and move further away from sin and back to the heart of God.

We need to constantly be running to the foot of the cross. We need to fall on our faces before the Living God and confess that we, left to our own devices, can quickly become wretched sinners. We must plead to be redeemed and ask for forgiveness. We must refuse to give in to selfishness and self-centered thoughts and understand the magnitude and potential of where our actions can lead.

We are no different than David. We cannot handle sin and temptation on our own. If we had that capacity, then there would have been no need for

Jesus to die on the cross. We are all in constant and desperate need of God's grace, mercy, and forgiveness. But most of all, we need God's love. We need to be attentive to His calling, following His Word and embracing His heart. David is a man after God's own heart, but he is not a perfect man.

Even David needed to carefully and intentionally maintain his relationship with God. Because we are flawed and our flesh is weak, we need to continually be handing over our thoughts and decisions to God and listening to His words. God doesn't expect that we will go through life without making bad choices. He merely asks us not to let them turn into incredibly horrible situations like the two described in this chapter. We can't ignore God and be successful in resisting temptation.

David is a man after God's own heart who does not possess the ability to prevent himself from breaking all of the commandments.

DYSFUNCTION

The pages of history are filled with stories of dysfunctional families. The Tudors in England had more than a few embarrassing moments. Almost the entire 16th century is full of their many depraved acts of immoral family dysfunction. Consider the family of Rodrigo Borgias (1430-1503). The second pope from that family, also known as Pope Alexander VI, was worse than his uncle, Pope Callixtus III, who was monstrously corrupt, even described by his closest allies as the "scandal of his age." Rodrigo was accused of buying the papacy, highly engaged in adultery, incest, theft, bribery, and murder. Arsenic poisoning became their favorite form of reducing the number of their enemies. Even while they are remembered as being great patrons of the arts, their dysfunction—though hidden for years—still existed and impacted thousands of lives.

One way or another, every family possesses some degree of dysfunction. Often dysfunctionality stems from the manner husbands and wives communicate and handle difficult situations. Many times younger couples just entering marriage find themselves challenged because they do not possess the tools required to manage the complications each of them bring into the marriage. Many marriages are carrying "baggage" from witnessing their parents interacting in the household growing up; we often find it requires years of dedicated professional counseling to set them free to start anew. If handled incorrectly, another generation will turn out like the last one, sowing and reaping the same complications along the way.

My mom and dad never argued, at least not in front of my siblings or me. As I have matured, I have come to understand they must have quarreled at times, but never in front of us. You might think that's a great way to grow up—but actually, the absence of witnessing two people disagree creates a dysfunctional understanding on the part of the children. Someone who grows up in a house where parents don't argue has no experience watching and learning how two people express a difference of opinion. Having grown up that way, my view of how a husband relates and interacts with his wife differed from Renee's experience. When she and I arrived at a point of disagreement, I would instantly shut down because I thought a husband and wife should never quarrel. I failed to relate in a healthy manner in those early years because I never engaged Reneé in any negotiations.

Parents who avoid talking about their differences in front of their children teach them an unintentional lesson: when you grow up, you should never disagree with your spouse. Alternatively, parents who battle each other in intense arguments in front of their children train them that there is no pleasant way to object and reach an agreement collectively. Children from dysfunctional homes often allow dysfunction to rule their homes, repeating the cycle. Conflict and poor communication almost always end with innocent people getting hurt.

While some dysfunctions are relatively minor and carry little consequence, not all family dysfunctions are benign. That's what we'll find out about David's household. King David had a total of nineteen sons (not counting the ones born to him by his concubines). He also had a daughter, Tamar.

Perhaps the most shocking and unbelievable dysfunction in David's family is found in the account of the events surrounding his oldest son Amnon, and the third-in-line, Absalom. Absalom has a beautiful sister named Tamar. Amnon finds his half-sister attractive and falls in love with her. The proper response to a potentially dangerous situation such as this one is painfully obvious—don't "go" there. Getting one's heart and head where it ought to be, and getting your half-sister out of your thoughts may sound like the only option. I think most people would hear alarms going off in their heads when a feeling like that enters one's mind. However, rather than purging his lust, Amnon chooses to continue daydreaming about Tamar and his fantasies about her increase. We read that they drove him to a point he made himself ill. Scripture says this about the situation, *"Amnon became frustrated to the point of illness on account of his sister Tamar, for she was a virgin, and it seemed impossible to do anything to her"* (2 Samuel 13:2).

Weeds are always easier to pull out of the garden when they are small. It becomes more challenging to pull them up when ideas such as this take root in our hearts and minds. Ultimately, we know what we should and should not be growing there, and yet we can't stop the progression because they have already taken root. In this case, Amnon appears to have lost any concern about right and wrong.

First Corinthians 6:18-20 says we should flee sexual immorality. We must pay attention to what the Word of God says here; it's not that He doesn't want us to have fun, it's because sexual immorality destroys us and those around us. That's the kind of destruction we see happening here with David and his family. Amnon is so downcast every morning because he can't have what he wants that his cousin Jonadab notices and tells him,

> *"Go to bed and pretend to be ill. When your father comes to see you, say to him, 'I would like my sister Tamar to come and give me something to eat. Let her prepare the food in my sight so I may watch her and then eat it from her hand.'"*
>
> —2 Samuel 13:5

Amnon takes his cousin's advice and asks David to have Tamar come and make special bread in front of him and then feed it to him—it would make Amnon feel so much better (and would allow him to be alone with Tamar in his chamber). What possibly could be wrong with a sister bringing her ill brother a home-cooked meal?

Tamar does what David asks of her. She brings the dough, kneads it, and cooks it in front of him—but once it is prepared, Amnon refuses to eat it. Instead, he exclaims, *"Send everyone out of here."* And then, he asks Tamar, *"Bring the food here into my bedroom so I may eat from your hand."* She complied. Amnon takes hold of her hand and says, *"Come to bed with me, my sister."* Tamar refuses and pleads, *"Don't, my brother!" She begs him. "Don't force me. Such a thing should not be done in Israel!"* We don't know whether Tamar is surprised by this or afraid. Either way, Amnon has no regard for his actions or Tamar. She includes him in her next plea, telling him he will look like one of the *"wicked fools in Israel"* (2 Samuel 13:9-13). However, her pleas and warning are unheeded.

The role of the family is to protect, care for, nurture, and support one another. The strong protect the weak; they don't prey upon them, take advantage of them, or use them. Amnon not only failed Tamar by his actions against her, but his disregard toward her sets off a series of detrimental consequences for his family. We must step up and play our role in the family as individuals. Every person must choose to refuse to allow themselves to be led by *"...the lust of your own hearts and eyes"* (Numbers 15:39). Matthew 26:41 says, *"Watch and pray so that you will not fall into temptation. The spirit is willing, but the body is weak."*

We see stories of "outrageous fools" all the time on social media. This type of behavior from celebrities and politicians seems to happen every day. Amnon and those who behave like him are following the "take whatever you want" attitude. Amnon learns this attitude from his father, David. David has set the example—as we learned in a previous chapter. David's actions speak louder than his words. By his behavior, David teaches Amnon to let his physical desires, fantasies, and his "needs" drive his actions.

What happens next? Amnon's lust turns to disgust. In what can only be described as a Jekyll and Hyde moment, we witness Amnon change his mind after the deed is done. *"Then Amnon hated her with intense hatred. In fact, he hated her more than he had loved her"* (2 Samuel 13:15). He demands that she leave his chamber. When she tells him sending her away is worse than the way he violated her, he calls one of his servants and has him throw her out and bolt the door behind her.

Now in the streets of Jerusalem, Tamar puts ashes on her head and tears her robe. Her brother Absalom sees her, and the first thing he says is, *"Has that Amnon, your brother, been with you?"* (2 Samuel 13:20b). Do we have to wonder—how does he know? In a truly dysfunctional family, sometimes people's attitudes and actions are pushed under the rug. Did other people pick up on Amnon's behavior towards Tamar before this day? Was David aware? We don't know the answers to those questions, but many times people ignore warning signs to "keep the peace" among dysfunctional family groups. Tamar's life is never the same. We only read that she is to live a miserable life in her brother's house. What was Absalom's reaction to this? Tamar is told (as too many women have been after an assault or rape), forget it happened; it will be better if kept silent. No wonder she lives her life out as a desolate woman. One can only imagine the heartbreak as her hopes and dreams of marriage and family—held from an early age, as with most young ladies of that time—are suddenly ripped away from her in one single moment of violent sexual aggression. Seeking a safe harbor and protection, she is not to find any consolation from her half-brother. Amnon fails in his role to defend his family. It is his responsibility to care for his family; he does the opposite for Tamar.

In John 21:15-19, Jesus tells Peter to follow Him and feed His sheep. Jesus is not referring to a literal flock of sheep, but His followers. Jesus has a deep love for us and gives Peter a command to take care of His people. As Christians, we demonstrate love for one another by tending to people in need. When we take care of the sick, the poor, and the needy, we are following Jesus. We live among people who are sick and vulnerable—spiritually and physically, just as in the days of King

David. In absolute contrast to this approach to life, Amnon does not care for Tamar but shows only contempt for her and his family when he gives in to his lustful desires and rapes her. He disgraces her even more by putting her out in the street when he could have asked to marry her. We need to realize the consequences of our sin often affect others, sometimes many others. For Tamar, she is to live in Absalom's house, "*a desolate woman*" (2 Samuel 13:20B).

One crucial thing we need to understand is that the consequence of sin is not equal to everyone. The effects of someone else's sin can render people wounded, weak, and defenseless. An excellent example of this is a husband who continually verbally, psychologically, sexually, and spiritually abuses his wife. The ramifications of his behavior will become apparent in the lives of his children, his family, and even their friends. Sexual immorality brings about some of the most dangerous dysfunctional results in the world.

While Absalom fails to defend his sister's honor publicly, he does see that Amnon pays for his sexual misdeeds. However, he takes the wrong path in doing so. Instead of doing the right thing, Absalom plots a deceptive plan of revenge and vigilante justice, which causes a great rift between him and his father, David.

It is more than five years before David forgives his son and allows him back in his presence.

Obviously, Amnon can not undo his crime. Not all offenders, however, behave as Amnon. While no excuse exists for doing something like Amnon did, we know some offenders become overwhelmed by guilt, shame, and grief over their sin. The offender may live the rest of his or her life trying to find peace and some way to redeem the shattered relationships with people whose lives they destroyed. On rare occasions, a kind of reconciliation can happen. Amnon, however, does not appear to be a repentant and broken man begging for forgiveness.

Dysfunction and sin, when left untreated, often lead to more dysfunction and sin, as it does in David's family. You see something is brewing all along in the heart of Absalom: he wants Amnon dead. It takes two years for him to execute his plan—a kind of family sheep-shearing festival. Discussing the celebration events with his father, Absalom encourages everyone to come. David refuses. However, Absalom insists that everyone attend. David says, *"All of us should not go; we would only be a burden to you"* (2 Samuel 13:25). And then Absalom specifically asks for Amnon to go. Can you imagine what David thought at that point? "Amnon?" David asks, *"Why should he go with you?"* (2 Samuel 13:26ʙ) Eventually, Absalom gets his way, and Amnon, along with the king's other sons, accept the invitation.

We're not surprised when we learn that Absalom tells his servants to pay close attention to Amnon. He probably tells them to make sure his cup is always full. You see, he instructs them to keep track when Amnon becomes drunk. Absalom tells them he will give them a signal, a signal for them to kill Amnon— and so they do. Absalom successfully has his men murder his brother Amnon. Afterward, all the king's sons mount their mules and flee the scene.

When news of the evening's event reaches King David, he is told Absalom has wiped out everyone. David is horrified. Jonadab, the cousin who had given Amnon the plan to rape Tamar, now enters the room and says only Amnon is dead, and it was Absalom who had arranged it. He says, *"This has been Absalom's expressed intention ever since the day Amnon raped his sister Tamar"* (2 Samuel 13:32).

What unfolds can best be described as a perfect storm of dysfunctionality. Let's have a roll call of the damage thus far: Tamar's life is ruined, Absalom is a murderer, David's heart is broken, and Amnon (the incestuous rapist) is dead. When will this madness cease?

David knows better; he knows what it looks like when darkness begins to descend on a soul. When unthinkable events and situations begin to transpire in his family, he should have stepped up rather than stepping back. He should have been the leader of the family who is driven to his knees. David should have led his family in begging for mercy from God for their wicked and immoral thoughts before those corrupt thoughts turned into evil actions.

Following Amnon's death, Absalom flees to another city. After three years, it is evident to Joab that David had come to grips with the death of Amnon and is missing Absalom, so Joab devises a plan to bring him back to Jerusalem. In 2 Samuel 14, Joab arranges for a woman to tell David a story in an attempt to restore the relationship between David and his son. Joab instructs the woman to dress in mourning clothes without any makeup and pretend that she is grieving. Joab intends to open David's eyes to this damaged relationship. The woman weaves a tale about having two sons who are not speaking to one another. After telling her story, David understands what she is talking about and realizes he should reach out to Absalom and not pretend that he doesn't exist.

We all need someone like Joab to be in our lives. Joab is a person who helps David see through the fog of complicated relationships and encourages him to do the right thing. Joab sees two men he cares about a great deal, stuck in a destructive cycle. Joab does not want to see David continuing down the path of destruction because of the way he handles his dysfunctional family relationships. He dares to confront David and tell him what needs to be done.

We all know people who are in dysfunctional relationships. We need to have the courage of Joab— the courage to confront people and possibly change the course of their life. But when faced with the decision of whether we want someone to be angry with us for a short time or for them to continue to live in denial or ignorance, we often choose the latter. We unknowingly become accessories to dysfunctional relationships. David's mishandling of family relationships creates the situation in which his family now finds themselves. David should have owned up to his wrongdoings many years ago. He should have taken the lead.

As Christians, we are called to live in what the Bible calls "community." This is why the Church exists. We should be actively encouraging and building each other up, helping one another get through difficult situations, and encouraging one another to do the right thing. If only David had done that in his life.

David agrees to allow Absalom to return home.
However, it is an empty gesture because, although
Absalom will be back, David refuses to see him face-
to-face. Now, David is in an estranged dysfunctional
relationship with Absalom. They live in the same town
for two years and never have any contact. Absalom
seeks reconciliation by contacting Joab and asking
him to arrange for him to meet with his father.

At this point, Joab has to follow the orders of his
king. He does not respond to Absalom's requests until
Absalom does something to get his attention. It seems
Joab has a farm which includes a plot of land adjacent
to land owned by Absalom. On that land, Joab has a
field of barley. Absalom has his servants burn it down.
When Joab approaches Absalom and questions him
about burning down his field, he has the opportunity
to request an audience with his father. Joab speaks
with David, and David agrees to meet Absalom. When
Absalom finally gets to see his father face-to-face, David
kisses him, and that's how the chapter ends.

I believe the silence between that kiss and the next
chapter speaks volumes. There is no mention of David
asking for forgiveness. There is no indication of his
remorse at the way he has treated his son. There is
no mention of David owning up to his part of the
preceding years; there is only a kiss. A kiss can say a

lot—it means I love you, yet it can also say I betray you, as Judas' kiss did to Jesus. Sometimes, however, it doesn't say enough. For enough to be said, there must be words of forgiveness, mercy, and grace, and always of honesty and transparency. Restoring relationships requires us to be genuine and not hollow in our efforts to rebuild. We have a responsibility to maintain and restore relationships among one another. When there are obstacles in our relationships with one another, there is an obstacle in our relationship with God. When our relationship with God is not in proper alignment, our life can collapse

Life is so much better when we do things God's way—especially with relationships. Some of us know people who are in a bad relationship. Perhaps we know someone whose marriage is in trouble. We need to confront them. It is better for them to be angry with us for a short time than for them to live in denial or ignorance. We should not allow their marriage to continue in a destructive spiral without at least attempting to work towards reconciliation.

Everybody is struggling on some level, but we would do good to understand that it is not always about being right, but being in the right frame of mind. This is connected to being in line with the Living God. One of the most important questions one can ask in a struggling relationship is, might there be a possibility that we are wrong? If we spend all our time and energy defending our position only to find out we are the one who is in the wrong, this not only accomplishes nothing, but increases our challenges and setbacks, and can easily result in a damaged relationship that it is more difficult to be restored.

Again, as followers of Jesus, we are called to live in community. This is why the Church exists. This call to community means we should encourage and build each other up so we can help one another see what is difficult for us to see within ourselves. In every relationship, there is ebb and flow, and when the times of ebb come, we have to help one another get back to the flow and find that sweet spot where enjoyment is possible again. But that takes work, a lot of work. We all need people like Joab in our lives.

Perhaps you know exactly what David is going through here. Maybe you are struggling in a relationship now that needs restoration. Or, perhaps you are struggling to do the right thing and battling temptation that seems to overwhelm you. Just as we see the consequences and ramifications of actions that we initially thought, "no one will find out," we know that is a lie. Our actions done in secret can have far-reaching results in the lives of people that we can't even imagine. When we don't do things God's way, we not only damage our relationship with God, but our relationships with one another, their relationships among themselves, and everyone's relationship with God is affected.

While this chapter ends with a kiss—a father's kiss for his son that's not quite enough—it's not quite the end of the story.

WE CAN DO BETTER

I t should have been more than a kiss (2 Samuel 15:33). After all that had transpired between David and his son Absalom, when both of them finally meet after years of estrangement, David should have done better.

Public figures are now, more than any other time in my life, the subject of more open discussion and social debate. Yes, we've had the media around for a long time covering the news and current events of the day. However, social media has opened up an entirely new way of viewing public officials and topics related in and around their lives and personal choices. In fact, I believe many of us can and do relate to this story.

As we read these passages about David in the Old Testament, it's easy to forget that these were current events at the time they were written. The general population is aware of David's issues, as we have been made aware of the inappropriate relationships and blunders of many of our leaders. Think about how public officials are treated when there is news of extramarital affairs, scandalous plots or other missteps. Consider how the Royals in Great Britain live under incredible scrutiny. Regularly followed by the media, everything they wear, do and say is analyzed by thousands of people daily. I believe the same was true in David's time.

If David's story were unfolding today, imagine all the memes and political cartoons we would see. Consider the famous "condescending" Willy Wonka Meme. Picture it saying, "So, King David, you saw a woman taking a bath—how did that work out for you?" Or The World's Most Interesting Man Meme, "I don't always pull married women out of bathtubs, but when I do, I make sure their husbands are pushed to the front of the line." Just think about all the modern devices that could be used to share David's experience in Jerusalem at that time.

How far does a relationship have to go to be as bad as the one between Absalom and David? Maybe David should have done more than simply kiss Absalom. Perhaps he should not only have begged for Absalom's forgiveness but sought forgiveness and displayed repentance before his entire kingdom. Unfortunately,

King David does none of those things. A public display of sorrow and regret is below him at this point. By the end of the story, he is full of profound grief, repentance and intense mourning. The ironic thing (on many levels) is, when Absalom comes back from his time in Geshur, David should have forgiven him instead of refusing to see him. He finally does forgive him—after it is too late.

As the story continues, we see that Absalom's plans do not include making up lost time with dad. He goes immediately from being kissed by his father, the king, to undercutting his authority. Absalom decks himself out at a time when horses were a novelty and reserved only for royalty. He makes sure he has the most beautiful horses and chariots of grand style for the day. Absalom arrives outside the king's residence early in the mornings (maybe because his dad is sleeping late). He holds court, playing on the declining popularity of his father. He begins settling disputes in a manner that is most pleasing to those bringing their problems for judgment. He artificially gains approval by manipulating the circumstances and bending them in his favor. Absalom engages in a conspiracy to make himself more agreeable to the people.

Needless to say, at this point in David's reign, his approval rating is at an all-time low. The people of Israel are not happy about David's exploits, his relationship with Bathsheba, or his plot to kill one of his own. I imagine the common men and women in the street are angry by David's abuse of power, authority, and privilege. One thing is certain, none of David's life escapes notice, and when someone makes these kinds of mistakes people love to share it with their community.

In a shocking twist in the plot, Absalom has a consult with David's long-time and trusted advisor, Ahithophel—the ablest and wisest political leader of the day. The conspiracy is quickly growing. Why in the world would Ahithophel come to Absalom's side and assist him in overthrowing the king? How is Absalom able to secure confidential advice from one of the king's oldest and most trusted relationships? The answer to this mystery may be revealed in the genealogy.

A careful study of the genealogy shows Ahithophel to be the grandfather of either Bathsheba or Uriah. There is some debate about the relationship. Either way, no grandfather would want to have a grandchild treated the way either one of those people was treated by David.

Ahithophel's first advice to Absalom seems shocking to our ears, as it should. How far, how deep, and how low does one have to stoop to take the advice Absalom receives from Ahithophel? What did Ahithophel suggest? He tells him to go and sleep with his father's concubines on the rooftop so that everyone in the streets and surrounding buildings can know what is happening. This suggestion is not random. To understand why this advice would even enter into anyone's mind, we must realize that during this time in history, when a king dies, the succeeding king inherits the former king's concubines.

I am sure you see the conflict. David isn't dead. Absalom commits this series of actions as a sign of aggression towards his father intended to humiliate him on many levels. These actions do not merely demonstrate disrespect of David's "property," but humiliation to the people. One has to wonder (and I am engaging in pure speculation here) if maybe David had a better relationship with these concubines than he did his own children. Ahithophel continues to advise Absalom. Scripture says something about Ahithophel that must be read:

> *Now in those days, the advice Ahithophel gave was like that of one who inquires of God. That*

was how both David and Absalom regarded all
of Ahithophel's advice.

—2 Samuel 16:23

As a legal advisor to the king, Ahithophel's words
were never questioned or challenged. Yet, if we are
not careful, we might miss the very important phrase,
"...like that of one who inquires of God." Don't miss
this. Ahithophel's advice had always been considered
wise—similar to, but not as one who speaks the truth
of God. Now that he's scheming with Absalom to
take the throne from his father, there is no more truth
or wisdom in Ahithophel's counsel. His words sound
right to Absalom, yet they have become anything but
the truth. How many times have we given or received
advice that sounded good but in reality, had no basis
in the wisdom and knowledge of God? This is a very
dangerous path and leads to ever darker places and
actions.

Now it gets interesting, as if things were not already
interesting. But now we have a new twist. Ahithophel
advises Absalom to choose 12,000 men and send
them out that evening in pursuit of David. In 2
Samuel 17:2-3 Ahithophel says,

> *"I would attack him while he is weary and weak.*
> *I would strike him with terror, and then all the*

people with him will flee. I would strike down only the king and bring all the people back to you."

It is said that this plan seemed good to Absalom and all the elders of Israel. It's hard to imagine that King David is now the subject of an assassination plot by his most trusted advisors, the elders of Israel, and his own son. How much of this could have been avoided? At what point could David have made a public confession? Why did David merely kiss Absalom, rather than seek reconciliation?

In our own time, we have seen celebrities and politicians engaged in the most outrageous and sometimes immoral behavior. Among those, we sometimes see public confessions and signs of repentance, outright denials of any guilt at all, or simply silence as their fan base diminishes, their constituents move to other candidates, and their followers fade. David is like the last of these. Everyone knows about his behavior. Yet, Scripture implies that David remains silent and does not speak out in public or with his family about any remorse or regret of his deeds and the impact they have on others.

Then Absalom does something unexpected. The great advisor, Ahithophel, must have been the most surprised when Absalom summons Hushai, another of King David's advisors, to analyze his advice. In 2 Samuel 17:7, Hushai says, *"The advice Ahithophel has given is not good this time."* He goes on to explain that everyone knows David is a seasoned warrior, and his men are the fiercest fighters around. Hushai warns Absalom that David's men are likely to attack first, leaving Absalom defeated and humiliated. Hushai advises Absalom that he should gather all the people together and lead them into battle himself. This approach will result in victory over David's men. If David tries to flee to a city, they will hunt him down and kill him. What Absalom does not know, however, is that Hushai has been sent by David as a spy. So Absalom takes Hushai's advice over Ahithophel's, and says with all the people of Israel, *"The advice of Hushai the Arkite is better than that of Ahithophel"* (2 Samuel 17:14). What a shock this must have been to Ahithophel.

Shortly after meeting with David, Hushai notifies Zadok and Abiathar, the priests still loyal to David, of the advice given to Absalom. The priests send their sons Jonathan and Ahimaaz to get the message to David by having a female servant girl carry the intelligence report. However, someone saw what was taking place and informed Absalom. It must have been like a scene from ancient Mission Impossible as the two spies hide in a well covered with a cloth on which grain is spread as if it is being dried. The search party sent out by Absalom does not find them. The woman tells Absalom's men they went across a brook, sending them in the opposite direction. Now David receives the news from his spies, and all David's people cross the Jordan and are not where Absalom expects them to be. In the meantime, Ahithophel becomes so distraught by the fact his advice is not followed that he hangs himself.

"David mustered the men who were with him and appointed over them commanders of thousands and commanders of hundreds" (2 Samuel 18:1). Imagine all these lives engaged in a civil war between a father and a son! David's men tell him not to go into battle with them, but remain in the city because he is *"worth ten thousand of us"* (2 Samuel 18:3), and they convince David to stay in the city.

Finally, we see David speaking out for his son. His only request to his soldiers is that they *"Be gentle with the young man Absalom"* (2 Samuel 18:5). David asks his generals to make sure they go easy on his boy. We've all seen the commercial where the father is talking to his daughter about being careful when she drives the car by herself, last-minute instructions to a new driver. As the camera pans back, we see a four-year-old girl sitting in the seat. And then the camera flashes back to a teenage girl who says, "I know dad, I'm gonna be careful." As parents, in times of crisis, we are prone to remember our children as they were when they were young. Perhaps this is why David refers to his son as a young man.

The casualties that day are great—twenty-thousand men. The battle is spread out over the whole countryside, and the forest swallows up more men that day than the sword. The territory here is composed of rocky thickets. It's not a territory that's conducive to anyone in a hurry. What a terrible mess this is—what a horrible landscape of corpses must have been laid out as far as the eye could see. The number of the dead compares to the bloodiest battle of the American Civil War, the battle of Antietam in Sharpsburg, Maryland. It is the bloodiest one-day battle in American military history.

So, the army of David goes out to fight against the army of Absalom. David's mighty men are victorious that day. When they find Absalom, he is hanging in an oak tree in midair. As Absalom is traveling through the forest on a mule, it goes under the thick branches of a great oak tree. His beautiful head of hair is caught in the oak, and he is *left hanging in midair while the mule he was riding kept on going"* (2 Samuel 18:9B).

One of the men tells Joab about Absalom's fate in the tree, and Joab responds,

> *"What! You saw him? Why didn't you strike him to the ground right there? Then I would have had to give you ten shekels of silver and a warrior's belt"*
>
> —2 Samuel 18:11

But the man responds to Joab telling him that even if he felt in his hand the weight of ten-thousand pieces of silver, he would not reach out his hand against the king's son; it was in our hearing the king commanded you to protect Absalom (Abbreviation mine). Joab says, "I'm not going to wait like this for you" (2 Samuel 18:14). He then takes three javelins in his hand and thrust them into the heart of Absalom while he is still alive, dangling with his head caught in the oak tree. Joab's armor-bearers, ten of them, surround Absalom and strike him as well. I suppose enough was enough, and Joab has had enough of Absalom and the trouble he stirred up among the people. Perhaps he is wondering how many more lives would be lost due to this conflict between father and son. It is possible he thought this was a battle that would never end until one of them was dead.

Thus, the wild career of David's son Absalom ends. He is loyal to his sister, yet he becomes a treacherous

enemy of his father. He is skillful at winning the favor
of all of Israel, yet foolish enough to believe he has
the allegiance of David's most loyal friends, including
his father's trusted advisors. We shouldn't be surprised
that Absalom constructs a monument to himself;
he does not have a son to carry on his name, but he
wants people to have something to remember him by
(2 Samuel 18:18, Paraphrase).

If anyone had reason to be a rebellious child, it
was Absalom. However, the lesson here pertains
to personal responsibility and respect for parents.
Absalom could have, theoretically, broken the cycle of
deceit, lies, mean-spirited, and humiliating behavior.
Returning evil for evil is like gouging an eye for an
eye repeatedly—eventually, everyone is blind! Too
many have had less than ideal home situations. Far
too many have had abusive, deceitful, and unloving
parents. Yet plotting revenge or death of your parents
brings more harm to you and your life than it will
theirs. Absalom failed to get satisfaction and lost his
own life in the process.

Joab casts the remains of Absalom into a great pit
in the woods, and soldiers throw a large heap of
rocks over him. Even though Absalom had built the
elaborate monument to himself, Scripture records
that his tomb stood empty for centuries outside

Jerusalem. The location that is now called Absalom's tomb is almost certainly a construction from later Roman times.

The news reaches David as he is sitting between the gates of the city; a watchman tells the king a messenger is approaching. Then another messenger is seen running behind him. The first messenger tells the king that all is well and that the enemies have been defeated. When David asks about his son, the messenger says he doesn't know what was going on; there was some commotion happening, but he does not have any details. When the second messenger comes with the same news, David asks him about his son, and the messenger answers, *"May the enemies of my lord the king and all who rise up against you for evil be like that young man"* (2 Samuel 18:32). The king knows his son is dead.

What a tragedy that David is weeping and mourning for Absalom now that he is dead. I believe he would have been better served by grieving for his sin, and the consequences of his decisions upon his family and country. This day of victory was said to be a day of mourning. How much greater it would have been if he had shed tears of repentance than tears of grief and loss. David covers his face and cries out: *"O my son Absalom! My son, my son!"* (2 Samuel 18:33b). When

Joab comes in the house, he says to David,

> *"Today you have humiliated all your men, who*
> *have just saved your life and the lives of your*
> *sons and daughters and the lives of your wives*
> *and concubines. You love those who hate you and*
> *hate those who love you. You have made it clear*
> *today that the commanders and their men mean*
> *nothing to you. I see that you would be pleased*
> *if Absalom were alive today and all of us were*
> *dead. Now go out and encourage your men. I*
> *swear by the Lord that if you don't go out, not a*
> *man will be left with you by nightfall. This will*
> *be worse for you than all the calamities that have*
> *come upon you from your youth til now."*
> —2 Samuel 19:5-7

Joab does not hold back but speaks the truth. In the annals of literature, there are only a few places where we see and hear such brutal and painful honesty delivered to a king, commander, or ruler. It almost bears a second reading. Can you imagine facing one of the fiercest warriors who has ever ascended to the throne and delivering a speech like the one Joab did?

If you have been following along up until this point, you're probably wondering how God or anyone could think so highly of David? Let's put that question on hold for a moment as we wrap up the story recorded in 2 Samuel.

Absalom's rebellion is immediately followed by a troublemaker named Sheba, son of Bicri, a vain and ambitious rebel from the tribe of Benjamin (the tribe of Saul). David now turns his attention to defeating this revolt of tribal disputes that amount to nothing more than power plays and rhetoric. The king appoints his nephew, Amasa, the son of David's sister Abigail, as the commander of the impending battle. When Amasa is late to meet David, he appoints another nephew, Abishai (the son of David's sister Zeruiah), and with *"Joab's men, the Kerethites and Pelethites and all the mighty warriors"* they went out to pursue Sheba (2 Samuel 20:7). When Amasa finally catches up with them in Gibeon, he must not realize how much he has become hated because of his slowness to mobilize the army against Sheba. Joab *"takes him by the beard as to kiss him,"* but stabs and kills him. Then Joab and his brother Abishai continue in their pursuit of Sheba.

Sheba finds himself in full retreat and attempts to take refuge in a nearby city. When Joab begins to annihilate everyone in the city because they offer Sheba safety, the citizens save themselves by throwing Sheba's head over the wall. Thus ends the revolt by Sheba. Once again, in this final battle we see David reaping the seeds of discontent with another rebellion

and more relatives of his house murdering one
another. David's family is an extremely dysfunctional
one.

David did not lead as righteous a life as someone
known for loving God would seem to lead. He didn't
have any commandments left; he broke them all.
In the case of David, we have one who fails at every
point. How guilty does that make him? How can it
be said that he is a man after God's own heart? He
sinned and sinned in a big way. However, consider
what James has to say concerning the Law: "*For
whoever keeps the whole law but fails in one point has
become guilty of all of it*" (James 2:10).

David's story is everyone's story. It is the story of the
complex choices and behaviors that are nothing more
than the sinful actions that follow from the sinful
thoughts and desires of the human heart. In David's
life, we see his deepest struggles that mirror our own.
Whereas in the life of Jesus, we see how God becomes
man; He walks in real shoe leather. Our redeemer
knows what it is like to be fully human. Yet, Jesus
knew no sin during His time on earth. David, on
the other hand, fails in more ways than many of us
combined, and yet he receives this title and honor
from God Himself. Rather than asking "why" or

"how in the world," we ought to say, "Thank you, Lord!" Because we know there's room for hope and room for grace for us if we follow David's example. Psalm 51 reveals the greatness of David. Here you'll find the history and the thoughtful words of the man after God's own heart, and the broken heart of a sinful man revealed.

David knows how to repent. While he knows how to disobey, he is much better at obeying. He understands God's nature and character. He fully comprehends God's mercy and knows how to receive that mercy and forgiveness better than anyone else in Scripture. Understanding God's mercy and grace is perhaps one of the most difficult things to grasp. In this lies the mystery of the epic life of David. He is unafraid to admit his transgressions. His own sin causes him suffering so great as to break his own heart. It is not the ugliness of his sin or the depth of his failure that makes him great, but instead the struggle and earnest desire to be accepted and forgiven by God's grace.

In 1 Kings 2:1-4, we are told of David's last words to his son Solomon, the heir to the throne. Pay close attention to these words as you read them:

> *When the time drew near for David to die, he*
> *gave a charge to Solomon his son. "I am about*

to go the way of all the earth," he said. "So be
strong, show yourself a man, and observe what
the Lord your God requires: Walk in His ways,
and keep His decrees and commands, His laws
and requirements, as written in the Law of
Moses, so that you may prosper in all you do and
wherever you go, and that the Lord may keep His
promise to me: 'If your descendants watch how
they live, and if they walk faithfully before Me
with all their heart and soul, you will never fail
to have a man on the throne of Israel.'"

I pray that we all hear it. First, these are the words
of a man who is still pursuing God. Yet, as we listen
carefully, we will surely also hear the instruction of
a man who understands that this pursuit is a daily
endeavor—a daily denying of self and taking up the
cross and following. David's life was never a perfect
response to God, yet it was a life that knew where and
how to find mercy and grace to help him get back up
and, once again, pursue the Father's heart.

All of this mercy and grace is available to me, and
you. We must despair over our sin but not despair
over God's mercy and grace if we truly and earnestly
repent and seek to know and love God the way David
loved God. You can see it if you look closely enough;
David was not a man with God's heart; he was a man
after God's heart. Do you hear it? He is in pursuit

of God's heart, he wanted to have it, but he wasn't quite there. When we look at David closely, what we see is a man running to God's heart—often falling down but ever getting up, dusting himself off, and beginning the pursuit again. Having a heart after God's heart is not a perfect heart—it is a heart that values the mercy, grace, forgiveness, and love of a Father who picks up His child and says with love that echoes through the ages, "Get after it again."

It took me a long time to understand that David didn't have a heart like God's, but he wanted one more than anything. And so, David's legacy is that three-thousand years after his life, he is remembered for his earnest repentance, his deep abiding love for God, and the fact that Jesus acknowledges Himself as the "son of David." This is indeed a testimony of the greatness of his epic life. Among mortal, fallen humanity, there is no life more epic than that of David.

EPIC LIFE

CONCLUSION

First, I hope you have a new appreciation for what it means to be a man or woman after God's own heart. We are all called to pursue a heart like God's—a heart for God like David's. Our Heavenly Father loves us more than we can imagine. Discovering the true potential of a relationship with Him should compel us to wake up each morning yearning for an even deeper experience.

We are all pretty much alike in the way we rebel and act out when things don't go the way we want or think they should. In fact, I came away from this writing with a renewed awareness of how much we all desperately need a Father to love us and a King to lead us. Like David, when we get knocked down, we need Him to be there to pick us up and bind our wounds.

Finally, I hope you now know your life is—and can continue to be—an epic life. If you truly know the One who transforms the ordinary into the epic, you will experience this transformation when you commit to the Disciple life—the denying oneself daily, taking up your cross and following Jesus. You see, David's epic life is a life marked by the pursuit of the Father. The best way for us to do this is to follow the heart of the One who indeed has a heart exactly like the Father. David himself longed for the day when he would see and know that One, Jesus, who lived the most epic life of all.

Do you desire an epic life? We have everything we need—it's already at our disposal. We have the example, and we have the direction. You may be asking yourself, How will I apply this to my life? The answer depends on who you allow the master planner of your life to be. It is interesting to me, in examining the epic life of David, we can see a pattern: when David is doing things on his own, he fails; when he follows the Father, he rises above. The key is: to follow, to pursue, to go after. That is why I continuously say some of the most comforting words in Scripture are, "*Come, follow Me*" (Matthew 4:19, Mark 10:21, Luke 18:22). These words speak to the pursuit, the going after. They also speak to the fact that it will be our King and Savior who does all the hard work.

David eventually gets there. In one of his last Psalms (139:14), he writes, "*I praise You because I am fearfully and wonderfully made; Your works are wonderful, I know that full well.*" It is interesting to me that most of us miss the part, "*Your works are wonderful.*" That, my friends, is the heart of the epic life, and it is my prayer that you live one. Follow the King, and you can.

ACKNOWLEDGEMENTS

I would like to thank the following people for helping make this book possible: My good friend Michael Cooley and my assistant Theresa Howard for their many hours of dedication and work on this project.

I also want to thank my staff: Jason Bowen, Rand Burton, Alexis Coelho, Rusty Guest, Dylan Higgins, Ian Larson, Rex Wiseley, Tiffany Bullington, Cathi Geerlings, Joy Hulsey, Marisa Runnals, Megan Smyth, Laura Stout, and Beth Smith. And the church elders: Willie Alexander, Hank Carter, Jim Dressler, Chester Gunnin, David Halm, Curtis James, Chris Larson, Ron Williams, and Von Woods, for all their encouragement and support.

Most of all, I thank my Lord and Savior, Jesus Christ, who gave His life so that we might have eternal life with Him.

EPIC LIFE

ABOUT PEACHTREE CITY CHRISTIAN CHURCH

In 1972, a group of people gathered in the newly
constructed Peachtree City Elementary School
to worship as the Peachtree City Christian Church.
Since those days, a lot of growth and change
has occurred for both the city and the church.
Through it all though, some things have remained
steadfast: PTC3's (as the church has become known)
commitment to Christ, His message, and the desire
to be a valuable part of the community. These have
remained steadfast because of PTC3's dedication
to her Mission and Vision to Build Relationships,
Introduce People to Jesus and Grow Disciples
(Mission), and to be a praying church that impacts
our families, community and the world. (Vision)
This commitment has led her to provide ministry in a
variety of different areas, which demonstrates PTC3's

dedication to living out the Great Commission. Examples include taking a team to Jesus Place Inner City Mission every month since 1993, and construction of homes and two churches in Ghana, Africa. Since the year 2000, PTC3 has sent a team to Guatemala every year, and—as of 2019—built a church, 80 homes, done medical missions work, and a variety of other Church programs. PTC3 has sent teams to the Apache Nation, Haiti, and Mexico, as well as several other countries. PTC3 continues to support local efforts such as Christian City, Promise Place, Bloom, Square Foot Ministries, I58, Fayette Samaritans, Midwest Food Bank, and others. In addition, PTC3 is committed to having a welcoming campus space for the community—making space available to a variety of ministries and groups.

George would like to invite you to come and see what PTC3 is all about. If you can't make it to our campus, please check us out online at ptc3.com, download our free app, and watch us live during our weekly broadcast on Sunday mornings at 9:30 and 11:00.

Made in the USA
Columbia, SC
01 July 2020

13036084R00067